GERMAN SHEPHERD FACTS

Kalyn Barnette

GERMAN SHEPHERD FACTS

Copyright: Published in the United States by Kalyn Barnette

Published November 2020

All rights reserved. No part of this publication may be reproduced, stored in retrieval system, copied in any form or by any means, electronic, mechanical, photocopying, recording or otherwise transmitted without written permission from the publisher. Please do not participate in or encourage piracy of this material in any way. You must not circulate this book in any format. Kalyn Barnette does not control or direct users' actions and is not responsible for the information or content shared, harm and/or actions of the book readers

German Shepherd

The variety was once formally recognized as the "alsatian wolf canine" inside the unified realm from after the essential world fighting until 1977 while its title used to be changed lower back to german shepherd.An disdain of its wolf-like look, the german shepherd is a pretty present day type of canine, with their starting district dating to 1899. As a grouping canine, german shepherds are working canines developed at first for crowding sheep. Taking into account that time, notwithstanding, because of the truth of their energy, knowledge, teachability, and dutifulness, german shepherds round the area are often the supported variety for parts sorts of artistic creations, for example, insufficiency help, look for and-salvage. German shepherds are medium to huge estimated pups. The variety well known apex at the shrinks is 60–65 cm

(24–26 in) for grown-up guys, and 55 60 cm (22–24 in) for females. German shepherds are longer than they're tall, with a top notch level of 10 to eight 1/2. The akc official variety smart does not, at this point set a trendy weight variety.[10] they have a domed brow, a protracted square-lessen gag with durable jaws and a dark nose. The eyes are medium-sized and earthy colored. The ears are huge and stand erect, open on the front and equal, yet they much of the time are pulled again toward movement. A german shepherd has a delayed neck, which is raised while energized and decreased when moving at a fast movement just as following. The coat is notable in assortments: medium and extended..The long-hair quality is latent, making the long-hair range more uncommon. Treatment of the extensive hair model varies all through necessities; they're broadly wide-spread anyway not rivaled the present covered young doggies under the german and joined realm pet hotel golf hardware simultaneously as they can rival sizeable ensured canines, anyway are respected a flaw inside the american pet hotel participation. The fci notable the long-haired kind in 2010, show it on the grounds that the reach b, while brief-haired kind is recorded in light of the fact that the reach a. Most typically, german shepherds are each tan/dark or ruby/dark. Most extreme shading sorts have dark veil and dark body markings which can go from an ordinary "saddle" to an in general "cover". More uncommon shading variants comprise of the sable, normal dark, regular white, liver, silver, blue, and panda assortments. The all-dark and sable sorts are directly in agreement to most prerequisites; nonetheless, the blue and liver are viewed as serious shortcomings and the all-white is reason for immediately preclusion from appearing in compliance at all variety and subject matter shows. German shepherds had been reared especially for their knowledge. In a rundown of breeds generally plausible to bark as guard dogs, stanley coren positioned the variety in second area. Combined with their power, this quality makes the variety legitimate as police, gatekeeper and look for and salvage doggies, as they're in a capacity to quickly inspect various obligations and decipher bearings better than particular varieties

Made in the USA
Middletown, DE
17 June 2021

42452236R00020